CALIFORNIA BIOGRAPHY SERIES

Pioneer Women
of
California

CALIFORNIA BIOGRAPHY SERIES

Pioneer Women of California

Linda Lewin

Toucan Valley Publications, Inc.

Copyright © 1999 Toucan Valley Publications, Inc.

ISBN 1-884925-81-2

Illustrated by Jean Tamminga.
Cover illustration depicts the *Madonna of the Trail* statue honoring
pioneer women, located in Upland, California.
Photographs of Nancy Kelsey and Elizabeth Gregson are courtesy of
the California History Room, California State Library, Sacramento, California.

No part of this book may be reproduced in any form, electronic or mechanical,
without the written permission of Toucan Valley Publications, Inc.

Available from:
Toucan Valley Publications, Inc.
PO Box 15520
Fremont CA 94539-2620

Phone: (800) 236-7946
Fax: (888) 391-6943
E-mail: query@toucanvalley.com

Web site: **www.toucanvalley.com**

Manufactured in the United States of America
First Edition

Pioneer Women of California

	Introduction	7
1	Nancy Kelsey	9
2	Elizabeth Gregson	17
3	Margaret Hecox	25
4	Tamsen Donner	33
5	Biddy Mason	39
	For More Information	47

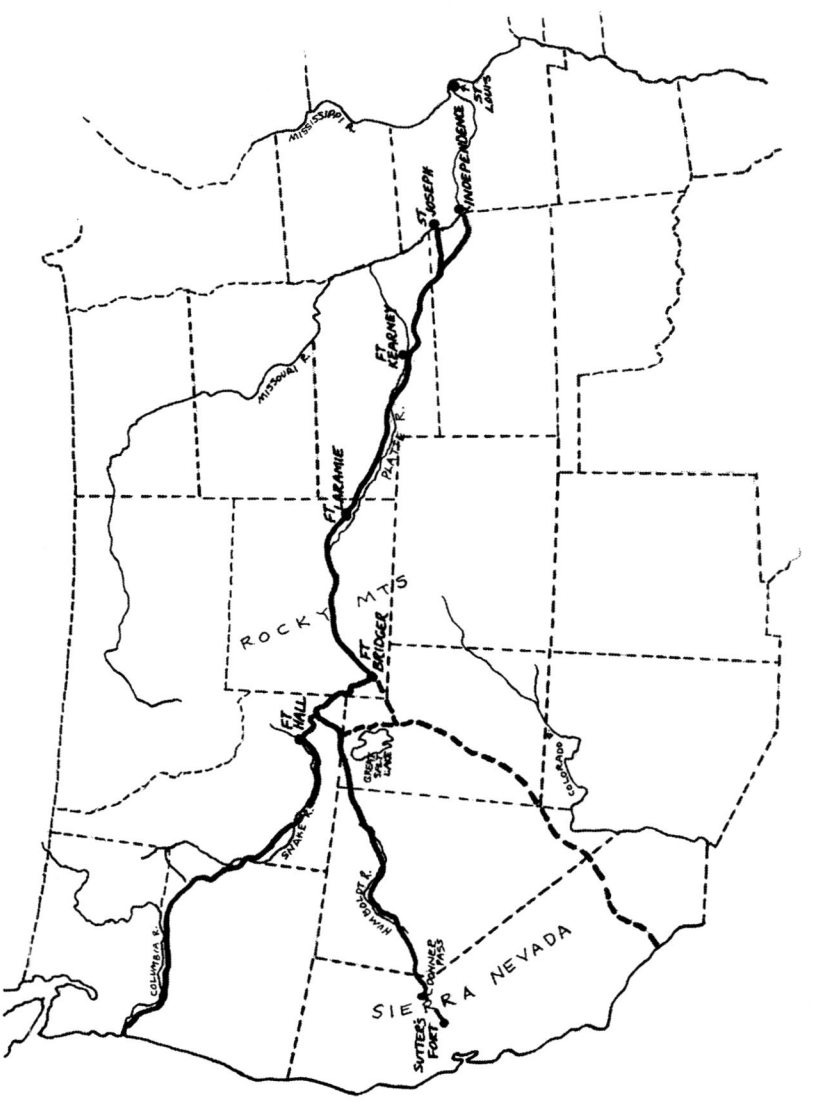

Pioneer Women of California

They left the comforts of the known for the uncertainties of the unknown, always hoping for a better life for their families in a new place.

The pioneer women of California in the mid-1800s were those who crossed the continent to reach the west. These American women faced two great challenges: the journey itself, which was thousands of miles and many months of rough travel over almost uncharted trails; and the task of recreating their familiar eastern lifestyle in a country without schools, churches, and towns such as they had known.

Earlier, the pioneer women of California were the Mexican wives who came with their husbands to settle near the first forts and build the first *pueblos* (villages). And before the Mexicans, the Indian women made homes for their families in the wilderness of California.

Margaret Hecox, one of the pioneer women of California, told her story to Marie Valhasky, who wrote it down and published it in *The Overland Monthly*, 1892. Margaret wrote:

"It seems to me that nothing like as much has been written about the women who crossed the Plains in early days as about the men. I suppose the reason is that those women were not the kind who wrote books, or even talked much about themselves. They were generally too worn out to complain, but if any one of them could tell all she felt it would make a large volume."

What we know about those women who came to California in the 1800s comes mostly from diaries and letters that they wrote. Their experiences show the individual struggles of life in California when it was a new state.

The time of the covered wagon trains inching across the prairies from Independence, Missouri, and over the mountains and deserts to California began about 1841 with a few families. It peaked soon after 1849, when gold was discovered and hundreds of women followed their husbands west. Completion of the railroad across the continent in 1869 changed the manner of travel and sped up American settlement of California.

Nancy Kelsey

(1823 - 1896)

Nancy Kelsey was the first American woman to enter California from the east. She crossed the plains and the Sierra Nevada mountains in 1841. (Mrs. Joel Walker had entered California three weeks earlier by way of Oregon.)

Early Life

Born in Barren County, Kentucky, on August 1, 1823, Nancy Roberts moved with her family to Jackson County, Missouri, when she was three years old. She grew up on the frontier near Independence, Missouri. She was only fifteen when she married 25-year-old Benjamin Kelsey, an adventurous young man from Kentucky. At sixteen she gave birth to their first child, Martha Ann. Two years later she lost a baby. Nancy and Benjamin were living from hunting and farming, and having a rough time.

The Kelseys Head West

Since he was interested in adventure, it is not surprising that Ben and his family joined his brother, Andrew, and other Kelsey family members in the Bartleson-Bidwell wagon train heading west in May 1841. Some were bound for Oregon, others for California, all in search of new opportunities. Nancy Kelsey was still a teenager when she, with her infant daughter, chose to make the trip to California. She was the only woman in that party of 32 men. When asked why she was making such a hard journey with a baby, she replied, "Where my husband goes, I go. I can better endure the hardships of the journey than the anxieties for an absent husband."

The party endured many difficulties. They had to abandon their wagons near the present-day Utah/Nevada border and most walked the rest of the way. Nancy walked barefoot, carrying her baby and leading her horse. She was pregnant with her second child.

While crossing the Sierra Nevada, the group stole some Indians' stash of acorns, and ate them without leaching out the poison. Ben nearly died from cramps. Later they had to kill one of their horses for food. Then Nancy collapsed when they got to the San Joaquin Valley. Amazingly, everyone was alive when they finally reached the John Marsh ranch east of San Francisco on November 4, 1841.

Settling in California

In San Jose they had to obtain Mexican passports. They went by boat up the Sacramento River to Sutter's Fort. Like many of the new settlers in California, they were offered a place to live and employment by Captain John Sutter. Benjamin worked seven weeks for Sutter, whipsawing lumber. While at the Fort, Nancy gave birth to a son who lived only one week.

Benjamin began hunting and trapping with his brother, Andrew. They sold deer and elk hides. In April 1842, the Kelseys left the Fort and traveled to the Napa Valley. They built a cabin near present-day Calistoga. About a year later they had saved enough money to buy a herd of cattle. Ben decided to drive the cattle to Oregon and settle there. They went all the way to Fort Vancouver on the Columbia River. Nancy gave birth to another child, a girl, in Oregon. They sold many of their cattle for money to live on.

Nancy Kelsey

A few months later, Ben wanted to return to California, so Nancy and her children were traveling again. They went back to their cabin in the Napa Valley. There Benjamin worked for Mexican General Vallejo building a sawmill. It was on Sonoma Creek near Mission San Francisco de Solano, which had been founded twenty years earlier. Vallejo, the mission commissioner, built Pueblo de Sonoma in 1835. It had a group of adobe houses in a square, with a plaza in the center. General Vallejo was very kind to the settlers.

The Bear Flag

American settlers in California were beginning to want independence from Mexico, and conflicts were flaring up. Unaware that the United States was already at war with Mexico, some settlers declared a California Republic. On June 14, 1846, Benjamin Kelsey and his brothers took part in the Bear Flag Rebellion. They joined a group of Americans led by Captain Ezekiel Merritt. They attacked General Vallejo's fort at Sonoma, captured eighteen Mexican officers, and stole a large quantity of arms and ammunition. Then Captain John Frémont came from Sutter's Fort to take command.

Nancy Kelsey worked as a cook and seamstress for Frémont's volunteers at the fort. She later reported that she and two other women sewed the original Bear Flag with cloth that they supplied. Mrs. Abraham Lincoln's nephew, William L. Todd, drew the bear and the star in the corner. He printed the words "CALIFORNIA REPUBLIC" just above a red strip of flannel.

According to some, the bear was chosen because of Benjamin Kelsey's frequent encounters with bears. One of the people viewing the flag is reported to have said, "A bear stands his ground always, and as long as the stars shine, we stand for the cause." The Bear Flag was soon replaced by the American flag as the U.S. occupied California during the Mexican War. In 1911 the design was adopted as the official California State flag.

After the war ended, Ben Kelsey worked for General Vallejo with a crew operating a sawmill on Sonoma Creek. Nancy cooked for the workers. At this time, Andrew Kelsey and his friend, Charles Stone, bought a ranch from General Vallejo's brother, Salvador Vallejo. The General and his brother had seized the land for the ranch from the Pomo Indians. The land was adjacent to a beautiful lake. The Kelseys called it Clear Lake, and later founded the town of Kelseyville there.

In the spring of 1848, when the Kelseys heard of James Marshall's discovering gold, Ben (and probably Andrew) went mining a few miles east of Coloma. They called the spot Kelsey's Diggings (later known as Kelsey). The gold mining was successful.

With his gold, Ben bought a herd of sheep and resold it at the high price of $16,000. He continued to mine and, using Indians as slave laborers, soon dug almost a million dollars worth of gold. Then the brothers and their friend, Charles Stone, bought more livestock and drove it back to the Clear Lake ranch.

A Massacre

However, in the winter of 1849, Andrew Kelsey and Charles Stone were not so lucky. The Pomo Indians around Clear

Lake had endured enslavement and harsh treatment from the settlers. One morning when Stone came out of his house, it was surrounded by Pomo. They shot arrows at him. One arrow entered his stomach and killed him. Kelsey tried to run but was also killed. Then the Indians fled to an island in the lake to hide.

When Andy and Charley didn't show up at Sonoma in the spring to visit Nancy and Ben Kelsey, they feared an Indian revolt. They asked the army to investigate. Samuel Kelsey joined a volunteer group led by Captain Nathaniel Lyons. They found Stone and Kelsey dead. They also found Indians on the island, though these may not have been the attackers.

The army sent for two whaleboats and two cannons. Men in the boats approached from behind the island and started shooting at the Pomo. They killed about 100 men, women and children. This was the worst massacre in the history of California. The island became known as "Bloody Island."

Many years later the lake was partially drained. On part of the old William Edmunds Ranch on Highway 20 there is a plaque that reads:

>Bloody Island
>Scene of a Battle Between
>U.S. Soldiers Under Command of Captain Lyons
>and Indians Under Command of Chief Augustine
>April 14, 1850

More Journeys

Nancy's husband, Ben, always had the wanderlust, and so the family never remained in one place very long. She and her children accompanied him to several different locations in the west. In 1850 they went to Humboldt County, where they may have helped establish the towns of Eureka and Arcata. From there they returned to their cabin in Napa County. There Nancy had her seventh child, a girl.

In 1856 they lived in Kern County. Ben was involved in building a bridge across the Kern River. In 1859 they traveled to Mexico, and two years later they went to Texas. There they were attacked by Comanche Indians. The women and children were home alone at the time. They hid in a shallow cave. One of Nancy's daughters, Mary Ellen, was hurt when she was caught by the Comanches. She died six years later from the injuries she received there.

In the 1860's the Kelseys moved to Fresno County. They later relocated to Puente, a Los Angeles suburb, and then to Los Angeles. Benjamin passed away there at the age of 75, on February 17, 1889.

Nancy, at age 65, now traveled to Cottonwood Canyon near Cuyama Valley to be with her oldest daughter, Martha Ann, and her family. They helped her build a cabin, where she raised chickens.

Later Years

A reporter interviewed Nancy Kelsey at age seventy, at her cabin home in the Cuyama Mountains in 1893. When the reporter left for Santa Barbara, she asked to go along with him. It was a sixty-mile trip in a buckboard on mountain roads. Although it took ten hours, she did not complain of fatigue.

In that same year Nancy was diagnosed with cancer. She lived three more years and died on August 9, 1896. She was 73 years old.

Her grave lies on a former Indian camp near Cottonwood Creek, which goes into the Cuyama River. On one side of her lies her daughter, Mrs. Nancy Clanton, and on the other a grandchild. To commemorate Nancy Kelsey as the first pioneer woman to cross the mountains into California, the Native Daughters of Taft, California, erected a small marker at her grave.

Quote on page 10 is from Donovan Lewis, *Pioneers of California*, p. 281.
Quote on page 12 is from William Martin Camp, *San Francisco: Port of Gold*, p. 52.

Elizabeth Gregson

(1824 -1889)

Eliza Gregson felt that pioneer women had been neglected by historians. She therefore wrote her "memoirs" on the backs of old bills, letters and whatever other scraps of paper she could find. Her daughter, Mrs. Eliza Butler, copied them and her son, Dr. Chester Gregson Butler, had them published along with James Gregson's records as "The Gregson Memoirs" in the *California Historical Quarterly*, 1940. What we know about Eliza Gregson's life is based mainly on these memoirs.

Early Life

Eliza Gregson, named at birth Elizabeth Marshall, was born on March 15, 1824, in Manchester, England, to John and Anna Marshall. She was one of five children. Her father had difficulty supporting the family, as he was a gambler. He moved his family to Stockport and then to Derbyshire. There he set up a cotton yarn business, but it failed. At this point, in 1836, John decided to leave for America in search of a new opportunity.

His wife, Anna, and the five children remained in England. They moved to Hayfield, where there was a cotton yarn factory. Twelve-year-old Eliza and her older brother (age 14) worked there. The family just barely survived, eating mainly oatmeal mush three times a day.

Three years later, in 1839, Eliza's father was able to send for his family to join him. They happily sailed to the United States and made their home in Pawtucket, Rhode Island.

On October 20, 1843, Eliza married her childhood friend, now a 21-year-old blacksmith named James Gregson. After living with his parents in Philadelphia for a year, the young couple moved to Rock County, Illinois. They had 18 dollars--a lot of money at that time. Eliza soon gave birth to a son, who died before he was three months old. Eliza describes their small cabin. "...there [were] holes in the sides that you could throw [your] hat through....Was it any wonder that we were sick or that our [baby] died [?]"

The Trip West

In the spring of 1845 the family heard about free land in Oregon and decided to head west. Most likely they traveled on the Oregon Trail, starting near Independence, Missouri.

By the time they got to Fort Hall on the Snake River they had run out of supplies. So they joined another party traveling west and worked for them. The group's leader was Elija Bristow. James drove their oxen and Eliza did the cooking and washing.

On the way, the Bristow group met a party heading to California and looking for recruits to go with them. Eliza and James decided to change their destination to California. They joined this wagon train, led by John Grigsby and William Ide. There were about fifty wagons in the party, guided by Caleb Greenwood.

Everything went smoothly up to Truckee Meadows (now Reno, Nevada). There Indians killed many of their oxen and other livestock. Having only two oxen left, the Gregsons could no longer pull their large wagon. They made a small cart from it for supplies, and everyone walked from there on. It was a long, hard haul up the mountains near Truckee Lake (now Donner Lake). They rested two days at the summit, and then traveled on.

"Well, we still kept up the march day after day, ever watching and looking for the promised land. [A]fter many days myself with some other young folks climbed up a very steep mountain and there standing under a Manzinita bush we saw the valley below [stretching] far and wide like an ocean. [I]t looked beautiful to us, for we were tired and weary of the mountains, but we were still 3 or 4 days travel from it." They reached Johnson's Ranch (near present-day Wheatland) on October 20, 1845.

At Sutter's Fort

A few days later they arrived at Sutter's Fort (now Sacramento). Captain John Sutter had built the fort as a center for new immigrants to California, and he offered food and shelter to all who came. Other people at the fort with the Gregsons were Mr. and Mrs. Daniel Leahy and their two little girls, Mary Ann and Libby; the Allen Montgomery family; and a Mr. and Mrs. McDowel and their three little girls.

John Sutter put James Gregson to work cutting lumber at "Pine Woods." Later Gregson worked for Sutter digging ditches, since there was no fencing around the farm. He also worked in the blacksmith shop.

At the fort in 1846 Eliza gave birth to a daughter, whom they named Ann. Indians from miles around came to see Ann, the first white child born in the region. Eliza recorded that they were very poor and had no coffee, tea, milk, sugar or butter. She wrote that their clothes were patched so much "the original [piece] could hardly be found."

James and Elizabeth Gregson

While Eliza was at Sutter's Fort, Sarah Montgomery held the first quilting bee at her cabin near the "Pine Woods." Besides the few women living at the fort, others came from camps and settlements many miles away. About twenty people attended--mostly women. Sutter wrote in his journal on January 29, 1846, "All the people attended a quilting party at Mrs. Montgomery's."

Mexican-American War

In June 1846 James Gregson, along with other settlers, got involved in the Bear Flag Rebellion. The Americans helped capture Mexican General Vallejo and some of his aides and horses. Vallejo was held at Sutter's Fort.

Soon the Mexican-American War reached California. James Gregson joined Captain John Frémont's volunteers. Lt. Edward Kern was left in charge of the fort while Captain Frémont was away. Eliza Gregson, Sarah Montgomery, and the other women stayed at the fort. That winter was a very, very rainy one, and dry firewood was scarce, as were provisions. The women and children shared their meager food with each other. They managed to get by. Eliza held a reading and writing class for the women and children at the fort.

The new year, 1847, brought the terrible news of the Donner Party. The group of settlers traveling to California had been trapped by snow in the mountains at Truckee Lake. When messengers arrived with the news, Captain Sutter sent a rescue party with food. When some of the survivors were brought to the fort, Eliza and the other women helped take care of them.

At the end of the Mexican War, in the spring of 1847, James Gregson and other soldiers came back to Sutter's Fort.

Gregson's next assignment from Sutter was to help find some heavy millstones to build a grist mill. In late summer James became very ill with "Sacramento Fever" that was hitting many people at this time. The doctor was unable to cure him and said that he would die.

Eliza went out in the fields and tried to find some herbs that would help James. The cows had eaten all the grass and herbs; all she could find was cow manure. She thought, that manure contains the grass and herbs the cows ate. So she took the manure, wrapped it in cloth and boiled it. She gave the broth to James. He said "You want to poison me....I told him [No,] see me drink. With that he took the bowl with both hands and drank it all and went to sleep. [He] slept 3 or 4 hours but the fever was gone."

Gold!

After James's recovery, Sutter asked them to go to Coloma, where James would help construct a sawmill and Eliza would cook for the workers. On the day they were to leave, according to what James later wrote, James Marshall came to the fort with a small bottle of gold. Gregson records this as the beginning of the great California gold rush, though dates and descriptions by others differ.

While in Coloma the Gregsons began to do gold mining. "...the men [stopped] working on the mill [Everything] was gold crazy. [Runaway] sailors and [soldiers] came into the mines. [My] mother & two brothers & my sister came to hunt for gold....[In] 1848 goods began to [arrive] in the mines & every kind was very high [priced:] flour $1 per pound, coffee $10 per pound, tea, $18 per pound ...eggs $18 per dozen....We [women] folks took in all the sewing such as [making] overalls. We could make $10 per day."

They were doing well until James became ill again in late 1848. Meanwhile Eliza had another daughter, Mary Ellen. When the girls became sick, too, the family left the gold mining area and moved to the Sonoma region. There Eliza supported the family by doing laundry and sewing. With the spring (of 1849) good health returned and James went mining again. But, once again, he got sick and had to come back to Sonoma.

A Farm for the Gregsons

In 1850 James and Eliza and her brother Henry took over a ranch in Sonoma County from John B.R. Cooper, a trader. The 160-acre ranch was in Green Valley. Now the family could farm their land and finally make a good living. James and the children stayed healthy for the next several years, but Eliza had an accident. Her husband's gun accidentally went off and shot her in the shoulder. It took her about three months to recover.

She gave birth to a son, John, in 1852. In 1853 the family moved into a log house that Gregson and his neighbors built. A daughter was born in 1854. Four more babies were born, one about every two years, until the Gregsons had eight children altogether. They farmed their 160 acres of land, planting orchards and vineyards and raising cattle. They were one of the first families in the Sonoma area to grow wheat. They lived at the ranch the rest of their lives.

Eliza and her husband are examples of how poor people turned their lives into successes in a new land. They were pioneers in farming in California. Eliza died on February 1, 1889. James survived his wife by ten years, and died on August 1, 1899.

Quotes are from "The Gregson Memoirs," *California Historical Quarterly*, 1940.

⌘ Margaret Hecox

(1816 - 1908)

When Margaret Hecox died, the *California News* reported that she "was one of the noblest women that ever breathed under the glorious skies of California. Her many deeds of kindness have been recounted not only in her home circle, but also by the rich and the poor, the strong and the weak, regardless of race..." (eulogy written by T. H. d'Estrella in *California News*, February, 1908.)

Early Life

Margaret was born in 1816 in Pennsylvania, into a large family. Her mother's family was German and her father's English. Margaret's ancestors on her mother's side had come to the United States in 1702 and settled in Reading, Pennsylvania. Margaret's father had been a soldier in the War of 1812. His father, Margaret's grandfather Hamer, had been in the Revolutionary War

"We were a loving and devoted family. We used to have such happy times, sitting around the large fireplace in the long winter evenings, cracking chestnuts and roasting apples. Father would tell us stories and mother would knit."

At age 19, Margaret married Reverend Adna Hecox, a widower ten years her senior. He had grown up in Michigan and was a leader in the temperance movement (the movement to make drinking alcohol illegal).

After moving around for ten years, they bought a 30-acre farm in Illinois. Margaret would have liked to settle down there permanently with her family, now three girls and one boy.

However, Adna had other ideas. He had been reading and hearing a lot about California, and thought it would be exciting to go there. Also, he felt a warm climate would help his poor health. In early 1846, despite Margaret's protesting, they sold their home. "I shed tears enough then and afterward to make a river to carry me back to my mother." They spent the winter preparing for a spring departure for California.

Off to California

In the spring they loaded their large homemade wagon. Later they found that the wagon was cumbersome and too heavy for the oxen to pull. They had to cut it down to a smaller size.

On March 23, 1846, the Hecoxes started out, joining three other wagon teams. In the party were Joseph Aram, his wife and three children, who were Mormons; Edwin Shaw; Charles Imus; Charles A. Imus, the leader; and John and James Taggart. Additional emigrants joined the party (now known as the Imus party) a little farther on.

Margaret gave each of her three little daughters a new doll she had made for the occasion. The girls were gleeful, but the baby boy was sick during almost the entire trip.

Along with the other women, Margaret worked very hard every day, into the evening, taking care of the children and preparing food for the next day. At night she would fall into bed, exhausted. Margaret was glad she had kept a mattress made of goose down on which to sleep.

They went overland from Illinois to St. Joseph, Missouri, arriving on May 3, and camped on the banks of the river. On May 8 the wagons were ferried across the Missouri River. After they crossed, heavy rain began and lasted for days. This slowed them down.

When the weather dried up, the men hunted wild turkeys along the way and the women cooked them. Recounted Margaret, "I roasted one of them before the fire so nicely that father [Adna] complimented me very highly, and the children shouted when they saw me bringing it to the wagon."

Troubles on the Trail

One evening when the family was camped between the Blue and Platte rivers, a huge swarm of big, black bugs came upon them. They looked like beetles and were about an inch long. The children were frightened when the bugs crawled inside their clothes and into their hair. The bugs crawled right into the meat Margaret was frying too. She ran with the children into the wagon, shooed the bugs out as much as she could, and closed it up. Meanwhile, the men were outside trying to keep the frightened cattle from stampeding. The next morning the bugs flew off as suddenly as they had come.

At Fort Kearny the party met a band of Pawnee Indians who camped near the wagon train. The Pawnees were friendly. The men talked to them and the women served them supper. The next morning the travelers gave the Pawnees some breakfast before they departed. After they left, the wagon party found that the Pawnees had "borrowed" many things. The men followed the Pawnees and got the stolen items back in exchange for some tobacco.

During the next leg of the trip, along the Platte River, Margaret was concerned about the illness of her baby son. Her husband, too, repeatedly got sick. At those times she had to drive the wagon, and wished some of the other men could help her more. "The women were different. We helped each other, and in sickness or trouble we could depend upon one another with as much certainty as if we had all been at home. Sometimes I think women are stronger than men. They never give out when a thing must be done."

Little Sarah Hecox received a pony for a present when her father traded a gun to an Indian for it. She enjoyed learning to ride it. The children had fun camping out and finding small treasures to take with them to California.

One day a herd of buffalo stampeded toward the wagon train. Margaret was in the wagon behind hers, taking care of a sick woman. When she saw the herd, she ran to her own wagon to stay with her children. She crawled under the wagon just in time, but somehow broke her collar bone. There was quite a scuffle and the men shot several buffalo, which provided meat to feed the party for a long time.

When they arrived at Fort Laramie, traders warned them that they should make friends with the Sioux Indians who lived there. The women prepared biscuits, bacon and coffee for the Indians. After supper, the Indians and the settlers smoked a peace pipe, thus agreeing that there would be no conflict. Young Sarah Hecox was delighted when one of the warriors gave her a pair of beaded moccasins.

Over the Mountains

The Imus party passed the Donner-Reed party along the trail. Unlike the Donners, Charles Imus decided not to take the new short-cut route, instead going by way of Fort Hall. In order to lighten their load for the last difficult part of the journey, Margaret had to part with some of her treasured belongings from Pennsylvania. For miles and miles they saw nothing but sagebrush. Then they gradually climbed the eastern slopes of the Sierra Nevada mountains in the hot sun.

During the ascent, Catherine Hecox got lost. Because of the steep climb, all the oxen were needed to pull each wagon, one at a time, while the people walked. When they stopped to rest they found that Catherine had disappeared. After about an hour and a half of hunting, the men found her at the edge of a cliff.

Shortly after this, Mrs. Aram and Margaret Hecox found what may have been some flecks of gold. They didn't know what it was at the time, and no one cared much about it.

The Imus party considered crossing the Sierra Nevadas near Truckee Lake (now Donner Lake), but then decided to take an easier trail, by way of Coldstream and Emigrant canyons. They finally reached Johnson's Ranch in the Sacramento Valley on the first of October, 1846. It was a barren place. "This is what we have traveled all this distance and endured so much to find," Margaret said to herself. "I looked about a while, then crawled into the wagon and cried until I could cry no more."

At Santa Clara

Just before they left for Sutter's Fort, most of the young men were recruited by John C. Frémont to fight in the Mexican War. Since the fort, now Frémont's headquarters, was very crowded, he suggested that the party head east to Santa Clara and stay in the abandoned Santa Clara Mission. A group of 57 emigrants, including the Hecoxes, spent the grim winter of 1846 secluded in this run-down, dirty building. One of the women organized a small school there for the children.

When the Mexicans threatened to attack the mission, the men had to stand guard 24 hours a day. But some were sick with typhoid fever, so the women had to help. Margaret wrote:

"I was always timid; a bug could frighten me into a spasm. I couldn't stand idly by, however, when danger threatened and my services were needed. I knew that if I couldn't shoot straight I could at least sound the alarm. The soldiers who were not sick were almost dead from lack of sleep. I put on my husband's hat and overcoat, then grasping our old flintlock between my shaking hands I went forth in the darkness to the corner of the wall assigned to me.... A terrible feeling of loneliness and desolation held me in its grip...."

Finally the U.S. Navy arrived and the Mexicans retreated. The war ended in January 1847.

A Home at Last

In the spring the Hecoxes were able to leave the mission. They decided to go to Santa Cruz. In the small village of Soquel, just south of Santa Cruz, Adna Hecox got a job helping to build a sawmill. Then they rented a building, and Margaret made it into a boarding house for the sawmill workers.

The following spring, 1848, they heard the news of the discovery of gold, and Adna Hecox took off on a gold hunting expedition. Before leaving he moved the family, which now had seven children, to Santa Cruz. Adna later became mayor and justice of the peace in Santa Cruz.

In 1869 a lighthouse was built at Santa Cruz. Adna was given the job of maintaining it. The family lived in the lighthouse for 46 years. After Adna's death in 1883, his daughter, Laura became the lighthouse keeper. Margaret Hecox lived at the lighthouse until she died in 1908. She was almost 93 years old.

Douglas Tilden (1860-1935), the acclaimed deaf-mute sculptor who created the Mechanics Monument in San Francisco and the statue of Serra in Golden Gate Park, was Margaret Hecox's grandson.

Quotes are from *The Overland Monthly*, vol. 19, May 1892.

Tamsen Donner

(1801 - 1847)

Of all the pioneer women who made the trip to California, Tamsen Donner was one of the most courageous and devoted to her family.

Early Life

She was born Tamsen Eustis in Newburyport, Massachusetts, in 1801 to William and Tamsen Eustis. Her mother died before she was seven years old, and her father remarried. She did very well in school, which she finished at age 15.

Tamsen became a teacher, first in Newburyport and then in an academy in Elizabeth City, North Carolina. While teaching there she studied French and fine art, and became very good at both. She also met and married Mr. Dozier. They had two babies but only a few years later, her husband and the two young children died.

A Teacher Who Knits

Tamsen returned to Newburyport for a time, then moved to Illinois where she got a job in a country school in Auburn.

When the school board members heard that she knitted while teaching, they asked her to choose between knitting and teaching. She insisted they come and observe her first. They found that the lessons were conducted very well, and no one was distracted by the soft clicking of the needles. She was allowed to continue knitting.

The next year Tamsen was asked to teach in a higher grade level school at Sugar Creek. There she disciplined some unruly boys and instilled respect in all her pupils. They called her their "little teacher," as she was five feet tall and weighed about 96 pounds. She also wrote stories and poems, which were published in the Springfield *Journal*.

While working at this school Tamsen met George Donner. He was a wealthy twice-widowed farmer, 62 years of age. She was 38 years old when she married George in 1839. They settled in Springfield, Illinois, and had three daughters. With George's two youngest daughters from his previous marriage, it made a family of five children.

Overland to California

Seven years later, the Donners decided to set out overland for California. George's brother, Jacob, his wife, Elizabeth, and their seven children went along. A third family, that of James Reed, went as well. Each family took three wagons. They packed so many things that the wagons were top heavy. Each wagon was pulled by eight oxen; horses, milk cows, and beef cattle walked along with them. Near Independence, Missouri, they joined with several other companies traveling west.

From a spot near the junction of the North and South Platte rivers on June 16, 1846, Tamsen wrote a letter to a friend.

"Bread has been the principal article of food in our camp. We laid in 150 pounds of flour and 75 pounds of meat for each individual, and I fear bread will be scarce. Meat is abundant. Rice and beans are good articles on the road; cornmeal, too, is acceptable. Linsey dresses are the most suitable for children. Indeed, if I had one, it would be acceptable. There is so cool a breeze at all times on the plains that the sun does not feel so hot as one would suppose.

"We are now 450 miles from Independence.... The prairie between the Blue and the Platte rivers is beautiful beyond description.... the Indians frequently come to see us, and the chiefs of a tribe breakfasted at our tent this morning. All are so friendly that I can not help feeling sympathy and friendship....

"Buffaloes show themselves frequently.

"I botanize, and read some, but cook 'heaps' more. There are four hundred and twenty wagons, as far as we have heard, on the road between here and Oregon and California...."

At Fort Laramie the group celebrated the Fourth of July with a big dinner. They exchanged gifts with a party of Sioux Indians. When the wagon train started out again, a group of about 300 warriors rode in pairs next to the wagon train, as an escort.

A New Route

At Fort Bridger, the party heard about a new route to California that shortened the distance by 300 miles. The trail (called the Hastings Cut-off after Lansford W. Hastings, a guide) went south of the Great Salt Lake and rejoined the Overland Trail on the Humboldt River.

They stayed at Fort Bridger a few days, arguing about whether to take the usual route or this new route. They could not agree. While most people took the old route, 87 people took the new. Going against the advice of those who knew the trails, they started south on July 28th.

After several days the people who went via the Hastings Cut-off found a letter from Hastings stuck in the bark of a stick. It informed them that the road ahead was in very bad condition. They had better go over the mountains -- and he left very scanty directions. At the end of September the group finally found the old trail on the Humboldt River, but all the other parties had long since passed and made the trip over the mountains.

Stuck in a Snowstorm

It was late October 1846 when the Donner Party started to cross the Sierra Nevada. Some wagons were abandoned as the snow deepened. A storm near Truckee Pass forced them to stop and set up camp at the lake (now Donner Lake).

The Donner families, six miles behind the others, stopped at Alder Creek when a wagon axle broke. George Donner cut his hand with his axe and was unable to travel further. They thought they had enough food for a month.

Donner's condition soon got worse. Some of the livestock died from starvation; others were killed for food. There still wasn't enough. Tamsen often went without eating so that her husband and children would have the scarce provisions.

The first rescue party reached the camps in mid-February 1847, bringing packs of dried meat and flour. They evacuated 21 people, including Tamsen's two oldest children. Both Tamsen and Elizabeth Donner refused to abandon their ill husbands.

A second rescue party arrived in early March. They found that Jacob Donner and several others had died. Those still alive were eating the flesh of the dead to survive. The rescue party started back with 17 people (including Tamsen's three youngest daughters), leaving 14 behind. George Donner was still alive, and Tamsen insisted on staying with him. Elizabeth Donner and four others died a short time later.

A third rescue party arrived and carried five survivors out. Only Tamsen and her husband remained at Alder Creek camp. Lewis Keseburg, who had a foot injury, stayed at the lake camp. A short time later George Donner died. His wife wrapped his body in a sheet.

Tamsen Donner's Death

When the last rescue party arrived in mid-April, they found only Lewis Keseberg. Keseberg said that Tamsen had died. He admitted that he was eating her flesh. Tamsen had told him about some money she had left at Alder Creek to be given to her daughters, and he had found the money.

The rescue team took Keseberg to Sutter's Fort. There he was accused of killing Tamsen Donner and another traveler named Wolfinger. Keseberg was found not guilty at a hearing. Many people, however, believed he was guilty.

Tamsen's children all survived. The two youngest daughters, Eliza and Georgia, were adopted by a Swiss couple, Mary and Christian Brunner. If the children's father had died earlier, their mother would have escaped with them. But Tamsen Donner was a brave and loyal wife who stayed with her husband till the end.

Many years later Donner Memorial State Historical Park was established a few miles west of Truckee. It includes the lake campsite. Visitors can hike to the Alder Creek campsite as well.

Biddy Mason
(1818 - 1891)

November 16, 1989, was declared Biddy Mason Day in Los Angeles. At the site of her original home, now a high-rise shopping center called the Broadway Spring Center, a special ceremony was held. Biddy's words, passed on from generation to generation, were recalled: "If you hold your hand closed, nothing good can come in. The open hand is blessed, for it gives in abundance, even as it receives."

Early Life

Biddy Mason was born in Hancock County, Georgia, on August 15, 1818. She was born a slave and her real name was Bridget. When she was very young she was taken from her mother and given to the family of John Smithson. Slaves were not permitted to learn to read and write. But as Biddy was growing up she was taught how to cook and clean and take care of livestock. She also learned about herbal medicine, nursing and midwifery (delivering babies).

When Biddy was eighteen, John Smithson gave her and three other slaves to his cousin, Robert Marion Smith and his wife, Rebecca. They had a plantation in Mississippi. Biddy had to take care of Rebecca much of the time, as she was sickly.

Rebecca gave birth to six children, probably all delivered by Biddy.

According to legend, Biddy married an Indian chief whom she may have met while gathering herbs. They had one daughter, Ellen, when Biddy was twenty. But she was actually not allowed to live with a husband, since she was a slave and had to stay with the Smith family. Later Biddy had two more daughters-- Ann, born about six years later, and Harriet, born four years afterward. Robert Smith may have been their father.

The Trip West

In 1847, Smith and his family decided to join the Mormon religion. The following year they joined a group of Mormons heading west to establish a Mormon community in Utah territory. They made the six-month trip from Mississippi to Utah by covered wagon. Biddy and her friend Hannah, another slave in the Smith family, had their children with them. It was Biddy's job to milk the cows every day, and to tend the cows, mules and sheep by walking with them behind the wagons. Biddy carried her baby on her back. The other slaves walked also. They were exhausted each night as they went to sleep in their tents.

The trip across the prairie was hot and dry. Biddy and her daughters wore bonnets to protect them from the sun and cloths over their noses and mouths to keep out the dust. Some of the cows died from the heat. Then, after a long, difficult journey through mountains and desert, they reached the Great Salt Lake. The Mormon settlers built log cabins and founded a community there.

Three years later, in 1851, Robert Smith joined a wagon train of Mormons who set out for California to establish an outpost. He took his strongest slaves, and chose Biddy Mason for her almost masculine strength. Once again Biddy walked behind the Smith's wagons to herd the cows and mules. There were more deserts and mountains to cross. Some of the oxen got too weak to work. Finally the wagons reached a valley on the other side of the San Gabriel Mountains in southern California. The Mormons settled in San Bernardino.

Freedom in California

After their arrival, Biddy began to think about freedom. California had been admitted to the union as a free state. Its constitution forbade slavery after September 1850. Biddy knew that some slaves had been given their freedom by their Mormon masters.

Smith did not want his slaves to hear about the freedom movement. Late in 1855 he loaded his wagons to move to Texas, a slave state. He took Biddy and her family and Hannah and her children. They had to stop in Los Angeles for supplies. At this time Los Angeles had a population of about 1,600, and only about a dozen were of African-American heritage.

There Biddy and Hannah got to know some other former slaves. Two young men were interested in Biddy's and Hannah's seventeen-year-old daughters. They wanted to prevent Smith from taking the slaves to Texas. Robert Owens, the father of one of the young men, was a successful horse trader. He went to the Los Angeles County Sheriff and got a court order for Smith to let his slaves go. He and his cowboys delivered it to Smith at his camp in the Santa Monica Mountains. The sheriff had Biddy, Hannah, and their children arrested for their own protection. They were cared for in the county jail.

In January 1856, Robert Smith lost the court case over ownership of his slaves. Slaves were not allowed to testify against whites in court. Judge Benjamin Hayes had to question them in his chamber, next to the courtroom. The judge ruled against Smith. Thus, five years before the outbreak of the Civil War, Biddy Mason, her friend Hannah, and their children became free.

Biddy's Special Skills

After being freed, Biddy and her family were invited by Robert Owens to live in his house. His friend, Dr. John Strother Griffin, gave Biddy a job as a nurse and midwife. She used the special medical skills she had learned when she was a slave. She took care of patients in the county jail and at the county hospital.

In 1857 Biddy's thirteen-year-old daughter, Ann, died of an infection. The following year her older daughter, Ellen, and her new husband, Charles Owens, had a son, Robert, and Biddy became a grandmother. Two years later, another grandson, Henry, was born.

In the 1860s, Biddy courageously nursed many people during a smallpox epidemic. Over the next two decades Biddy became well-known as a midwife, helping with the birth of babies and staying on several days to take care of the house and other children in the family. The use of herbal medicines was another of Biddy's skills. These skills had African roots, but Biddy had probably added to her knowledge from the Mormons, the Mexicans, and the Native Americans.

Becoming a Land Owner

Biddy worked hard and was very thrifty. Robert Owens, who had been acquiring land since 1854, may have advised her to purchase property. Over ten years she managed to save enough to buy a share in a large lot. Later, in 1866, she bought out the rest of the property, plus a second lot in the same block. Thus she became one of the first African-American women to own land.

Her land was on Spring Street between Third and Fourth Streets in Los Angeles. At this time South Spring Street was mostly a vineyard and settlement of adobe houses. Biddy may have built one or two wooden houses to rent out, but she did not live on her land until eighteen years later, when she was 66. Then she called her home at 331 South Spring Street "The Homestead." She made it a center for her extended family as well as a refuge for stranded settlers.

Biddy served people of all races and classes. Sometimes she served the poor, who could only pay her with some food. But she felt that one should give "with open hands and an open heart," as she said to her daughters.

In her home Biddy also held meetings to establish a church. In 1872 she and a group of friends organized the First African Methodist Episcopal (FAME) Church. Biddy helped pay the church's expenses.

Biddy's Business Sense Pays Off

Los Angeles was growing by leaps and bounds. Horsecars, stagecoaches and covered wagons filled the streets as newcomers continually arrived with their livestock. Hotels, schools, churches and a city hall sprang up. Biddy's skills enabled her to get higher paying work than most of the other

African-American women, who were mostly domestic servants.

In the 1880s Biddy bought four more lots from the Owens family in the block between Olive and Charity Streets. She decided to build a commercial building on some of her land. She rented out the first floor and lived above the stores. She also bought a six-story apartment building on South Spring Street. Gradually the Los Angeles financial district began to develop around her property, between Fourth and Seventh Streets. Her land became very valuable.

One part of her property Biddy gave to her grandsons, Robert and Henry, to open a livery stable. She sold some of her property and became a wealthy woman.

"If you hold your hand closed..."

Biddy used her money to help others. She became known as "Grandma Mason" as she worked in the worst slums in the city. She visited prisoners. She arranged for families made homeless by a flood to receive free groceries. "The open hand is blessed, for it gives abundance, even as it receives," Biddy said. Biddy also gave money to other churches.

African-American children were not allowed to attend public schools in Los Angeles at this time. The FAME Church rented one of their buildings to the Board of Education to use as a school for the African-American children of the area. But it soon closed because of the anger of the neighbors. Later Biddy started a private school and daycare center for all children in her neighborhood. She gave money to help fight the law preventing some children from attending public school. Eventually this law was changed.

Biddy and her daughter also opened and operated fourteen nursing homes in Los Angeles and San Bernardino. Biddy never stopped helping people in need. People who needed help formed long lines to see her at her home.

Biddy died on January 15, 1891, at the age of 73. She was buried in Evergreen Cemetery in the Boyle Heights section of Los Angeles.

Biddy's first building on the original property still remains, in the center of Los Angeles. It is part of the Owens Block. Her grandson, Robert Owens, inherited Biddy's apartment building. In a new building on this site he has set aside one floor as the Biddy Mason Memorial Institution, to serve African-American youth.

For More Information About Pioneer Women

Calabro, Marian. *The Perilous Journey of the Donner Party.* Clarion, 1999. (Gr. 5-8)

The Donner Party, a videorecording produced by Lisa Ades and Ric Burns. Steeplechase Films, 1992. (88 min.)
    See also web site:
    www.pbs.org/wgbh/pages/amex/donner/index.html

Ferris, Jeri Chase. *With Open Hands: A Story of Biddy Mason.* Carolrhoda Books, 1999. (Gr. 4-6)

Lavender, David Sievert. *Snowbound: The Tragic Story of the Donner Party.* Holiday House, 1996. (Gr. 5-8)

Levy, Jo Ann. *They Saw the Elephant: Women in the California Gold Rush.* Archon Books, 1990. (adult level)

Miller, Brandon Marie. *Buffalo Gals: Women of the Old West.* Lerner, 1995. (Gr. 5-9)

Robinson, Deirdre D. *Open Hands, Open Heart: The Story of Biddy Mason.* Sly Fox, 1997. (picture book)

Sigerman, Harriet. *Land of Many Hands: Women in the American West.* Oxford Univ., 1997. (Gr. 7-12)
    An excellent resource covering pioneer women from many cultures in a variety of careers, with historical photographs.

About the Author

Linda Lewin is a graduate of Douglass College at Rutgers University in New Jersey, where she grew up in a household where her parents published an educational magazine and filmstrips. Ms. Lewin has been an acquisitions editor at Simon & Schuster and, since moving to the West Coast in 1990, she has continued to do editing and writing, as well as teaching. She is the author of several children's books, a filmstrip series, and *Story Circle*, a series of multicultural storytelling videotapes.